MAKING AN
IMPACT IN
YOUR NEW JOB

MAKING AN IMPACT IN YOUR NEW JOB

The First 30 Days

Elwood N Chapman

**KOGAN
PAGE**

First published in the United States of America in 1990 by Crisp Publications Inc, 95 First Street, Los Altos, California 94022, USA.

This edition first published in Great Britain in 1990 by Kogan Page Ltd, 120 Pentonville Road, London N1 9JN

British Library Cataloguing in Publication Data

A CIP record for this book is available from the British Library.

ISBN 0-7494-0291-1
ISBN 0-7494-0292-X Pbk

Typeset by the Castlefield Press, Wellingborough, Northants.
Printed and bound in Great Britain by
Biddles Limited, Guildford.

Contents

About This Book

Making an Impact in Your New Job is not like most books. It stands out in an important way. It's not a book to read – it's a book to *use*. The unique week-by-week, self-paced format and the many worksheets encourage the reader to apply what is learned on a day-to-day basis in making her or his successful transition into a new work environment.

The objective of *Making an Impact in Your New Job* is to help new employees adjust successfully. Using this book will get you off to a faster start and enhance your career. Management will benefit from higher productivity, sooner. The book can be used effectively in a number of ways. Here are some possibilities:

Individual study. The book is self-instructional, all that is needed is a quiet place, some time and a pencil. It is recommended that the reader go over the entire book before reporting to work and then refer to it page by page on a week-to-week basis. Used in this manner, the book will take the reader through the first 30 days with fewer problems and greater success.

Workshops and seminars. After basic company rules, staff benefits, retirement plans, etc, are taken care of, *Making an Impact in Your New Job* can be passed to new employees to complete their induction. If only one or two hours are available, early pages can be discussed and the employee can complete the book on a day-to-day basis.

Open learning. Books can be sent to those unable to attend training sessions.

There are several other possibilities that depend on the objectives, training or ideas of the user.

One thing is certain: even after it has been read, this book will be looked at – and thought about – again and again.

Why 30 Days?

There are many reasons why a practical, 30-day improvement programme makes sense to ambitious career people. A few are listed below:

- Thirty days is long enough to demonstrate to yourself and your peers that you are making measurable progress in your job. It gives you enough time to demonstrate your potential to others.

- Thirty days is not so long that you or others will become discouraged by your progress and give up. You can focus your attention on your goals and reward yourself for reaching them.

- Changes in behaviour are usually achieved only after a strong commitment has been made. People are more apt to commit themselves fully for 30 days than for a longer period. For example, dropouts are not uncommon in 18-week college courses, but rarer in shorter courses.

- Another major advantage is that a 30-day period divides nicely into four weeks. Most career people plan their work and lifestyle on a week-to-week basis. This book is organised to take advantage of that excellent habit. At the end of each week you will review your progress and set new goals for the next week.

The 30-day system works. Give it a try!

To the Employer

Making an Impact in Your New Job was designed as a supplement and extension to any introductory programme for new staff. This book can help a newly appointed employee to adjust more successfully and completely. When this happens, there are several benefits to management, including:

- Higher productivity levels.

- Improved human relations. New employees will integrate themselves more smoothly into their respective 'teams'.

- Reduced employee turnover. Nothing will keep a new employee with an organisation longer than the pride that comes from being accepted, making a contribution, and receiving recognition for it.

For best results, *Making an Impact in Your New Job* should be available to new employees at the end of their induction training.

In those cases where a formal training scheme is not available or company literature in this area is limited, the book is recommended as an excellent substitute for an in-house programme.

To the New Employee

Thirty days from now, you will have become a professional member of the organisation you have joined (or missed out on an excellent opportunity). This book is designed to help you enjoy making progress in your new job without making unnecessary mistakes, so you can feel good about yourself. You should follow it page by page, week by week. You may wish to read the book right through and then reread it page by page as you work through your first 30 days in your new job. You should assess your progress at the end of each week and forms are provided to help you do this. It will then be possible for you to set goals for the following week.

A successful adjustment to your new job will give you greater confidence in yourself. Your new fellow-workers and superiors will also notice your progress, and when this happens, you will gain acceptance and recognition. You will know you have launched your career successfully. Good luck!

Elwood N Chapman

CHAPTER 1

Preparation:
Getting Ready for Your First Day on the Job

The challenge!

When you join a new organisation (or move into a new post) you become the 'new child in the class'. This means that all eyes will be upon you until you are accepted as a member of your new team. During this period, regular employees (including superiors) will observe your behaviour. They will be looking for answers to the following questions:

- How long will it take you to carry a full share of the workload? Are your skills up to par? Will you pitch in and help others? Will you work consistently every day?

- Will you be good at human relations? That is, will you be sensitive to the needs of those around you? Will you side with fellow workers who display a negative attitude, or will you 'play it cool' and treat everyone the same?

- How successful will you be at winning over those colleagues and superiors who are critical? Will you know how to handle their testing? Will you be able to stand your ground and win the respect of colleagues and superiors alike?

In 30 days, these questions and many others will have been answered. If you are successful, you will have demonstrated that you are a professional, and your fellow-workers will support and encourage your future progress.

You will have met the challenge!

Be a 'comfortable' person to meet

As a stranger to your new colleagues, it is only natural that you will be studied and reacted to. You will attract attention because you constitute a change in the work environment. Whether you transmit a favourable image or not depends primarily upon your friendliness and grooming.

To communicate friendliness, you need to be a 'comfortable' person to meet. This means avoiding the kind of behaviour that might make people think you feel 'above' or 'beneath' them. It is important to relax, smile and become a team-member without creating unnecessary waves.

It is also important to communicate a positive visual image by paying attention to your appearance (but without overdoing it).

To help you prepare yourself, some specific guidance on grooming is given below. Combined, these points constitute the physical image you will communicate. Assess yourself in each area by circling the appropriate number. A 5 indicates that no further improvement is possible. A 3 or below indicates that improvement is needed.

	High				*Low*
1. Hairstyle, hair grooming (neat/ clean)	5	4	3	2	1
2. Personal hygiene (clean finger- nails, etc)	5	4	3	2	1
3. Appearance of clothing (clean, pressed)	5	4	3	2	1
4. Appropriate shoes (clean, polished)	5	4	3	2	1
5. Choice of clothing (not too casual)	5	4	3	2	1
6. Choice of clothing (appropriate for the work environment)	5	4	3	2	1
7. Accessories (not too outlandish)	5	4	3	2	1
8. Once you are ready, look in the mirror. Is this how you want to look on your first day in the job?	5	4	3	2	1

Naturally, your attitude towards meeting new fellow-workers is the key. The moment they sense you have a sincere desire to join the group (and you are willing to make their jobs easier through your contribution) you will be on your way towards full acceptance.

Getting ready checklist

Before reporting for work, you will feel more confident and professional if you do the following:

☐ Buy a pocket notebook in which you can write special instructions, directions and names you need to remember.

☐ Be sure to make proper travel arrangements. Have you had your car serviced recently? Are you familiar with the bus timetable?

☐ Decide on the best route in order to avoid traffic problems and frustrations. Have you made advance arrangements?

☐ If you have a small child, work out the details of your childcare arrangements. Do you have a proper back-up? Will your arrangements allow you to concentrate fully on your job?

☐ If you have older children, will they be fully instructed on how to take care of themselves without telephoning you at work, except in emergencies?

☐ Cut back on outside commitments during your first 30 days. Would a weekend skiing or cycling trip drain you for Monday morning? Many new employees overreach themselves and miss a day's work when it counts most.

☐ Work out your wardrobe for the first week in order to present your best image.

☐ Adopt a regular exercise schedule.

☐ Take care of any necessary dental, medical or other professional appointments well in advance.

Through advance planning, professional people avoid asking for time off from their jobs. Especially during the first 30 days of a new job.

What to expect

It's happened! You are starting a new job that shows promise. What can you anticipate? On the left is the good news. On the right are some challenges you may face before the first week is over.

Good news	Challenges
Your employer has confidence in you or you would not have been selected in the first place.	You may be working for a demanding supervisor.
Your ability to contribute will be respected by your colleagues.	You may not receive all the help you would like or need.
Your organisation is keen for you to improve yourself.	Not everyone will welcome you with open arms.
You are a valuable asset and the more you learn the more valuable you will be.	Your new working environment (including the negative attitudes of fellow-workers) may not be everything you had hoped for.
You obviously have confidence in yourself or you wouldn't have accepted the position.	You may find you need to upgrade your skills in a hurry.
You will not be expected to work with maximum efficiency at the beginning.	There may be some pressures you did not anticipate.
You were probably hired as much for what you can learn as for what you already know.	You may discover you are more tired at the end of the day than you expected.

There is no such thing as a perfect supervisor, working environment or organisation. Your challenge is to make the most of what you find on a day-to-day basis and forge ahead. In 30 days, after you have had the opportunity to see the overall picture, you can make a more perceptive and accurate evaluation.

Learning the ropes

Every organisation has its own special culture. This means that the individuals who make up your new environment have their own customs, habits and performance standards. To be fully accepted into their world, you will have to honour their ways of operating and adjust accordingly. You must become part of the team in order to make a full contribution to productivity. If you isolate yourself, your contribution will be less than it should be.

How do your learn the ropes in your new environment? Here are three suggestions:

- Read all the company literature available. Study personnel procedures. Learn about company benefits so you don't have to ask unnecessary questions. Until you learn the rules, you cannot be a professional player.

- Learn the unwritten rules of the game; talk to people; be observant. What behaviour is tolerated but frowned upon? What behaviour would be approved by your supervisor but turn colleagues against you – and vice versa?

- Try to find out how new employees have excelled or got into trouble in the past. Ask your supervisor for feedback. Ask professional colleagues for suggestions. The idea here is to avoid typical traps that could cause your fellow-employees to reject you as a professional.

If you are fortunate enough to have gone through a well-designed induction training programme before reading this book, you are at a big advantage. Rethink what you learnt during the programme and then use *Making an Impact in Your*

New Job to put it into practice. If you did not attend a formal course, use this book as a guide to becoming a professional. Simply take things page by page and week by week until you are over the hill.

Be a team-player

When you start a new job, nothing is more important to your future than becoming a good team-player. What does this mean?

It has to do with *timing*. That is, being in the right place at the right time so that you can make your best contribution to the total operation of the department or team. There are three basic rules that will help to make you a good team member:

1. Before the work day begins you should arrive at work on time, in good physical shape, with an attitude that says 'I am ready to contribute'. Other team members don't have to hang around getting upset while you struggle to get started.

2. You should return from your breaks and lunch on time so you don't upset the flow of work. Other team members are not forced to answer your telephone or deal with questions about your absence.

3. You should get your work done on time. Other team members are not held up because your part of the job is being neglected. (For example, a waiter in a restaurant who is slow at clearing up and setting a table is not only causing customers to wait but also slowing down the entire team operation.)

Follow these rules and you will be a team member others can depend on. When you function in concert with fellow-workers (doing your part at the right time), everybody gains.

Doing a good job is important. Doing it at the right time is also important. The new employee who can accomplish both within a few days is the one who finds immediate acceptance among fellow-workers and superiors.

Understanding productivity

Regardless of the organisation (or new department) you join, your ultimate future will depend on your personal work output or 'productivity'. For the purposes of this book, productivity means the total contribution you finally make to your firm. And make no mistake – productivity is always measured!

It is relatively easy to measure the productivity of some employees, such as a salesperson, because results (sales) show up as numbers. However, the productivity of other employees, such as a flight attendant, is more difficult to measure. Intangibles, such as providing routine service to passengers and handling difficult situations, do not show up in any figures. Even when everyone's productivity is measured, intangibles are involved.

Different organisations assess productivity in different ways. They may concentrate on:

- Minimum acceptable performances – which may not always be clearly defined or communicated.

- Average performance – the mean of all employee productivity in identical jobs.

- Excellence – ie the degree of excellence that each new employee is expected to reach in time.

Look at the illustration on the following page.

There is a smaller gap between the expected norm and your potential productivity level. Once you match the performance of other employees, you should strive to get closer to your potential. Although there will always be a gap between what you could do and what you actually accomplish, the smaller the gap the better.

Learning attitude scale

Your personal attitude towards learning, more than any other factor, will be the key to your success during your first 30 days in the job. To help you become aware of this (and also to

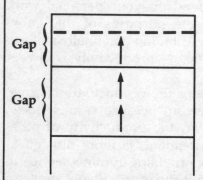

PRODUCTIVITY SCALE

Gap { — — — — — — — — — — —   Your potential productivity level

Gap {   Departmental norm (sometimes set by supervisor)

Starting level (first day on job)

You will notice that there is a large gap between the starting level of the new employee and the departmental norm – the average productivity of employees in similar jobs. Your challenge is to get your productivity up to the norm as quickly as possible. Depending on the job itself, this may take more or less than 30 days.

become more confident and positive), you should complete the following scale. Circle the number 10 if you agree 100 per cent with the statement. Circle a 1 if you are in total disagreement. Most people fall somewhere in the middle.

It is best to start a job knowing that you have plenty to learn.	10 9 8 7 6 5 4 3 2 1	It is best to rely on the knowledge you already have.
Do it their way until you *know* you have a better way.	10 9 8 7 6 5 4 3 2 1	Do it your own way until you're told to do it differently.
There is usually more than one way of doing a job right.	10 9 8 7 6 5 4 3 2 1	There is usually only one way of doing a job right.
Humility in a star performer is as important as in a beginner.	10 9 8 7 6 5 4 3 2 1	Humility in a star performer is unnecessary and ridiculous.
Learning during your 30 days can be more important than output.	10 9 8 7 6 5 4 3 2 1	Management doesn't care about learning, only about output.

Asking questions communicates a good learning attitude.	10 9 8 7 6 5 4 3 2 1	Asking questions irritates fellow-workers and makes you look stupid.
It shows a good attitude to say you want to learn.	10 9 8 7 6 5 4 3 2 1	Saying you want to learn demonstrates insecurity on your part.
Doing a job beneath your capabilities with a smile on your face shows you can take it.	10 9 8 7 6 5 4 3 2 1	Doing a job beneath your capabilities is demeaning and you should say you don't like it.
Admitting you need help is better than making mistakes.	10 9 8 7 6 5 4 3 2 1	Admitting you need help shows you are not capable.
You were hired more for what you can learn than for what you already know.	10 9 8 7 6 5 4 3 2 1	You were hired to do a job – nothing more, nothing less.

TOTAL [   ]

A score of 70 or more indicates that you know the importance of a learning attitude, no matter how much experience or education you may have. A score of under 70 indicates that you might get off to a better start if you use your first 30 days learning more and demonstrating less.

The first day

Can you remember the events that took place on your first day in your last job? Some people remember many details, even after 30 years have elapsed. Why is this?

The primary reason is because so much is at stake. You want to prove to yourself and others that you can handle things. You want to make the most of your new career opportunity. And you want to be accepted by your colleagues. No wonder most new employees are nervous.

The loyalty you may or may not feel after your first day is

very important. If you are ignored, shunted around or embarrassed, you may feel a resentment that can last for years. It may cause your attitude to be less positive. But if people go out of their way to be friendly and immediate bonding takes place, you are apt to become loyal and productive immediately. If your attitude is positive at the beginning, it will probably continue in the same way.

Your first day is so critical to your future that you can't afford to take chances. The following suggestions are made:

- Admit you are nervous, but demonstrate a sincere willingness to learn and adjust.

- Don't wait for others to be nice to you. Extend your own hand of friendship from the very beginning.

- Communicate an open, positive attitude through a smile and other gestures. When appropriate, enjoy a good laugh.

In other words, make your first day a success regardless of the difficulties you may face.

Wardrobe and grooming adjustments

On page 14 a few grooming suggestions were made to help you present your best image on the first day in your job. After getting the lie of the land as far as dress standards are concerned, most people make adjustments. Study the following examples.

- Estelle was more enthusiastic about her new office job than she expected, but she was not prepared for the sophistication and high-fashion image her colleagues communicated. Result? Estelle dressed from the top end of her wardrobe, took more care in coordinating her outfits, and devoted more time to selecting jewellery and making up her face. It didn't affect her work output but it made her feel more comfortable.

- In an attempt to make a good impression on his first day in the job, Greg dressed as if he was going to a wedding. He soon discovered that his department (drafting) was rather casual. Two employees wore jeans. Result? Greg took off his coat and tie and the following day (careful not to go too far) wore slacks, a conservative sports shirt and casual shoes.

- Jane accepted her new job knowing she would have to wear a prescribed uniform. The prospect didn't thrill her. Within a few days (after receiving more than one compliment) she discovered that the standard uniform emphasised her make-up and her hair. Result? She relaxed and decided to take advantage of the situation.

- James, accepting his first job in a department store, was amazed at the high standard of dress. In discussing the matter with his supervisor, he was told: 'It is not only what you wear but how you keep your hair and beard trimmed, cleanliness, and all that goes with it that is important here. Our customers are sophisticated and our management is demanding. I hope you can adjust.'

- In the first hour in her new job, Maria knew she was overdressed. Result? She carried it off well the first day, then slowly moved into clothes that were less fashionable, and more suited to business.

New employees should not feel pressured into buying expensive new clothes in order to feel comfortable in their work environment. In most cases, taking a new look at an old wardrobe, careful coordination, and special attention to hair and general appearance will do the trick.

Suggestion

Your general preparation is complete. You are ready to start your first week in the new job.

After your second day, read the next 15 pages using one of the following methods:

- Read and study all the 'Week One' pages at once.
- Read and study a few pages each night after work.
- Read all the 'Week One' pages in advance and then review them one by one during the week.

Whatever procedure you decide to follow for the first week, continue it for the next three weeks. Doing this will improve your progress and prevent you from making unnecessary mistakes.

CHAPTER 2
Week One:
Getting the Lie of the Land

Remembering names

Unless you work for a very small organisation, you will meet many people on your first few days in the job. If you try to remember everyone's name at once, you may become confused and be embarrassed. It may be best to remember a few each day. Most people find it a great help to write the name of each person they meet in a pocket notebook. This allows you to get the full name and the correct spelling. Most importantly, you will be able to refer to your notebook at night and recall the meeting, remember the face, and practise saying the name a few times.

Madelyn Burley-Allen in her book *Memory Skills in Business** advises using the following steps to remember names:

1. Have a positive approach.
2. Be interested in remembering each person's name.
3. Listen attentively and, if unsure of the name, ask for a spelling.
4. Form an association with something you are familiar with (perhaps with someone else who has a similar name).
5. Use the substitution process by substituting the name with a silly picture, or with something you're familiar with, such as:

   Ben – Big Ben
   Bill – Electricity bill

6. Link the silly picture to the person's name.
7. Repeat the name and substitution (or association) until you are confident you know it.

**Memory Skills in Business* is available from Kogan Page.

Give yourself a full week to learn the names of key superiors and immediate colleagues. If you learn and remember ten names the first week, you are doing well. By the end of your first 30 days, you should be able to expand your list to 30 or more names.

You can't learn unless you listen!

Effective listening is the key to success in any working environment.* Good listening is especially important in the first few days of a new job. You will be receiving instructions on organisational policies and procedures, as well as job instructions (what to do, how to operate new equipment, what your specific responsibilities will be, etc).

If you fail to listen in a new job, you may miss a safety instruction that could prevent an injury. If you fail to listen, you may make a mistake later that causes a key customer to go to a competitor. You may accidentally damage a piece of expensive equipment. Or you may miss out on an important benefit (such as profit sharing) for yourself. It pays to listen!

How can you improve your listening skills for the critical days ahead? Read the statements below and tick the appropriate box.

	YES	NO
1. I will listen to what is being said rather than evaluate who is saying it.	☐	☐
2. I will listen with my eyes as well as my ears.	☐	☐
3. I will refrain from interrupting until I am sure I have received the message correctly.	☐	☐
4. If I am not sure about the message, I will repeat it to the giver and ask if I've got it right.	☐	☐
5. I will write down complicated or particularly important messages for review later.	☐	☐
6. I will make sure I am in the best position to hear the message.	☐	☐

7. I will keep my nerves under control. ☐ ☐

8. I will concentrate and not just pretend to pay attention. ☐ ☐

9. I want to hear every message. ☐ ☐

10. I will be a patient listener. ☐ ☐

If you gave yourself 8 or more 'yes' answers, you appear to be ready for your first few days in your new work environment. Bear in mind that your supervisor and fellow-workers will know whether or not you are a good listener before the first week is over.

Telephone tips

There is a good chance that your new job will involve some use of the telephone, perhaps extensive use. Either way, telephone courtesy is important to your firm and your success. Ten basic but vital tips are listed below. As you go through them, bear in mind that one way to improve your telephone courtesy at work is to start practising some of these tips at home.

Tick off the items you need to work on:

☐ Hold the transmitter portion of the telephone directly in front of your mouth. If you hold it too far away you risk not being understood.

☐ Avoid indulging in conversations on the side during a telephone conversation. The person on the phone deserves your full attention.

☐ Never eat or drink while talking. If your mouth is full when the telephone rings, wait a few seconds before answering.

☐ Answer as quickly as possible. A maximum of three rings is a good average.

A Practical Guide to Effective Listening by Diane Bone is a useful book on the subject; it is available from Kogan Page.

☐ When you place a caller on hold to answer another line or take care of an emergency, ask for permission and wait for an answer.

☐ Put a smile into your voice. It's easy to do: simply remember to smile as you answer a call. Believe it or not, your voice will sound more friendly.

☐ Whenever possible, use the caller's name. It may also be appropriate to use 'Sir' or 'Madam' in conversations.

☐ Use these four answering courtesies: greet the caller; give the name of your organisation (or department); introduce yourself by name; offer your help.

☐ Do not rush the caller. Listen carefully before you give your answer.

☐ When you finish your telephone conversation, be sure to do one or all of the following: thank the person for calling; if it's a customer, let them know you appreciate their business; give an assurance that any promise you've made will be fulfilled; leave the other person with a positive feeling.

How much productivity in week one?

How much you produce (and prepare yourself to produce) is the key to early success in the job.

How fast should your productivity improve? Here are three strategies to consider:

Strategy 1: Modest productivity – maximum progress in human relations. This means that you operate slightly beneath your productivity capacity and concentrate on building good relationships with those around you.

Strategy 2: High productivity – minimum attention to human relations. Most of your energy goes into job tasks and only a small amount into building relationships. You do this because you feel others want you to carry your full load quickly, rather than make progress in other directions.

PRODUCTIVITY SCALE

Your potential productivity level

Departmental norm

First Week | Starting level

You will want to demonstrate measurable progress in productivity as soon as possible. In reaching for the departmental norm, however, do not neglect what you need to learn and don't ignore relationships with colleagues and superiors. It is the combination of productivity, learning and working relationships that will provide long-term progress. In most jobs, you will be expected to produce less at the beginning, so you usually have time to improve in all directions.

Strategy 3: Good productivity – good human relations progress. The idea here is to balance your progress in both directions – show above-average speed in reaching higher productivity and work on building human relations at the same time.

Your choice of strategies depends on various factors. These could include:

Instructions from your supervisor. Your boss may say something like this: 'We are behind schedule, so I would appreciate your concentrating on getting work out. You'll have time to deal with other matters later.'

Attitude of colleagues. Your fellow-employees may not give you the chance to build relationships with them until you demonstrate that you are a good worker and are willing to carry your share of the workload.

Customer involvement. If you have customer contact on the first day or so in your new job, remember that the customer comes first. Everything else, including relationships with others who also have customer contact, takes second place.

Quality starts on day one

Please study this statement, which was made by a capable employee during her first week in a new job.

> 'If I can get by in the first month, then I can settle down and make whatever changes are necessary for outstanding career progress. Management will not expect perfection from me at the beginning.'

What kind of work and learning attitude does she transmit? See if you agree with the reaction of the author.

1. A 'get by' attitude might prevent her from learning all that needs to be learned for future progress. It could also create a lower than necessary level of performance, which could lose her the respect of other team members before she finally gets round to demonstrating her potential.

      AGREE ☐   DISAGREE ☐

2. The intention to 'settle down' after the first month might mean that she starts off with poor work habits and sloppy performance. This could continue after the first few days are over. Such an attitude violates the principle: 'Do it right the first time.'

      AGREE ☐   DISAGREE ☐

3. The phrase 'management will not expect perfection' denies that work environments have standards. Superiors expect new employees to reach standards step by step. Translated, this means that they want to see progress towards reaching standards from day one.

      AGREE ☐   DISAGREE ☐

In the author's view, striving for quality is always a winning strategy. The sooner it starts the better. The only way to reach

acceptable standards at a later date is to practise quality from the start. The new employee should resist any pressure to get the job done at the expense of quality.

Completing the following exercise will reveal some additional aspects of 'quality control'.

Quality awareness exercise*

Consider each statement and mark it true or false, based on your current awareness of the quality aspects in your work and personal life. Answers and author's comments are listed on the next page.

TRUE	FALSE	
———	———	1. Quality means preventing problems rather than picking up the pieces afterwards.
———	———	2. Quality is seen in the little things as well as the big ones.
———	———	3. Most new employees want to do quality work.
———	———	4. Personal quality standards and business quality standards have little in common.
———	———	5. Customers, colleagues and superiors pay little attention to quality.
———	———	6. People who talk about quality are idealists, not realists.
———	———	7. Quality takes time to achieve.
———	———	8. Quality means conforming to a set of personal standards.
———	———	9. Company quality expectations are best communicated informally by word of mouth.
———	———	10. Quality requires commitment.

SCORE ☐

*The exercise is based on one contained in *Quality at Work* by Diane Bone and Rick Griggs, published by Kogan Page.

Answers 1–3. True. 4. False (employees with high personal standards are usually the ones who lead business quality programmes). 5. False (customers, and most supervisors and colleagues, are often particular about quality). 6. False (people who talk about quality are realists). 7–8. True. 9. False (it is best when quality guidelines come from the top, are in writing, and are agreed by employees). 10. True.

Pacing is everything*

Some new employees are so eager to succeed that they set a fast initial pace that leads them into trouble. They are so intense about making a good impression that they make unnecessary mistakes, offend colleagues, or end up with a 'flash in the pan' or 'eager beaver' image that they never live down.

Professionals set a slower, steady pace. They are not as concerned about where they are at the beginning as where they will be in 30 days' time. They know that it takes time to learn new tasks, build sound human relationships, and ultimately make a team contribution. They recognise that it is their responsibility to fit into the existing environment first. Only then will they be in a position to offer suggestions for improvement and contribute at a high level.

This guide is designed to demonstrate the kind of pace that will minimise mistakes and enhance your professional image. For example, you will be encouraged to increase your personal productivity at a pace that will take you higher without sacrificing human relationships. To accomplish this goal, it is recommended that you check your progress on a week-to-week basis. Take your adventure one day at a time, but consolidate your gains every week and then start again. To encourage this approach, each of your first four weeks has been assigned a goal or theme.

The ideal time to review your weekly progress, consolidate your gains and prepare your goals for the following week is when you feel most comfortable. In doing this, you may wish

---

Make Every Minute Count by Marion E Haynes is an excellent book on this subject, also published by Kogan Page.

to refer to your notebook, identify any problems that have surfaced, and talk things over with someone seriously concerned with your professional future.

Case Study 1
Rescue

Pat felt confident and pleased after the two-day induction scheme for new employees. However, she was not prepared for the sophistication, skill level and fast tempo found in the department to which she was assigned. By noon of her first real day of work, Pat viewed herself as underprepared, underskilled and underdressed. Fortunately, on her way to the company cafeteria one of her new colleagues, Sandra caught up with her and they had lunch together.

During lunch, Pat received many tips and suggestions. For example, she learned from Sandra that Mr Gregg, their manager, was in trouble with his superiors; that Jill who worked next to Pat spread rumours and was not to be trusted; that Mrs K, the senior programmer, was recently divorced and was working overtime to escape from her personal life. Sandra was so friendly that Pat began to feel more confident. She was pleased when Sandra suggested they meet after work for a drink. Sandra's closing remarks were: 'Once you get the lie of the land around here you will be able to protect yourself and survive.'

What appears to be happening? What mistake may Pat be making? What advice would you give her?

_____

_____

_____

_____

_____

_____

_____

_____

_____

_____

_____

See page 75 to compare your thoughts with those of the author.

You and your supervisor

Your most important working relationship is with your immediate supervisor. Three basic factors are involved in building and maintaining such a relationship: productivity, cooperation with fellow-workers, and communication with your boss.

Your supervisor is responsible for departmental productivity. As is the case with individuals, there is always a gap between what is accomplished and what could be accomplished within a department. The sooner you close your personal productivity gap, the more you will be respected by your supervisor.

Supervisors are rated by superiors on the size of their departmental productivity gaps so they appreciate it when the relationship you build with fellow-workers results in a better team spirit and greater productivity. Sometimes they will take the trouble to compliment you on your efforts in this area.

The key to a solid relationship with your new boss is open, two-way communication. This does not happen automatically: it needs to be built up over a period of time and sustained. But how do you start? What might you do in the first week of your job? Here are three possibilities.

1. **The supervisor communicates with you.** The chances are that your superior will initiate some form of communication,

often during your first week. Take advantage of this opportunity to ask questions or discuss any problems related to your work output (operation of machines, skills, etc). If you sense that you are unusually slow, say so and wait for feed-back that may help you to improve your output.

2. **You initiate communication.** Not all good supervisors are outstanding communicators. Some are often so busy that they forget to discuss matters with new employees. Don't be afraid to walk up to your boss and ask how you are doing. It is important for you to know; it is also important for your supervisor to know that you want to know. Any problems you do not relate in the first week will make things more difficult in the second.

3. **Wait for the right opportunity.** It might have been a hectic week for your supervisor or you may need more time to prove you can handle things. In any case, if you do not communicate much with your superior in the first week, make it a primary goal during your second week.

Relationships with colleagues

The best way to build a positive relationship with your supervisor is to build good working relationships with your colleagues. When you do this you are adding to the harmony of the working environment and making a double contribution to departmental productivity. You are contributing, and you make it easier for others to do the same!

How do you build strong relationships with colleagues? Here are three suggestions to get started.

1. **Be a comfortable person.** Unless you are friendly and communicate openly and often with your colleagues, you may make them feel uncomfortable. This, in turn, can be misinterpreted. Instead of the easy-to-know person you can be, colleagues may see you as stuffy, a loner, or someone who thinks he's too good for the job. Do not allow this to happen.

2. **Accept assistance graciously.** It may be necessary for you to learn important tasks from someone with far less education or a different background from you. Whatever the case, go beyond the standard 'thank you'. For example, you might say: 'You have been a terrific help,' or 'I'm really grateful to you.'

3. **Put the mutual reward idea to work.** Later on (after you have developed your skills fully) there will be many ways in which you can repay your colleagues by chipping in when they need extra help. In your first week (if it seems appropriate) you might consider baking a cake or buying some doughnuts as a thank you for those who helped you through your first few days.

The 30-day humility scale
Surveys show that the biggest mistake new employees make is to flaunt their education or previous experience in a new work environment. Nothing annoys fellow-workers and superiors more than a know-it-all who does not appear willing to learn.

The following test has been devised to help prevent you from falling into this trap. Indicate whether you think each statement is true or false and check your score.

TRUE   **FALSE**

———   ———   1. No matter how much you know, your input will not be automatically accepted as valid when you start a new job.

———   ———   2. The higher your academic background, the easier the adjustment to your new position will be.

———   ———   3. It's better to behave modestly than to make a humiliating mistake because you didn't listen and learn.

———   ———   4. To have a good learning attitude even someone with a PhD needs a degree of humility.

———— ———— 5. To be less assertive than usual is never a good idea on a new job.

———— ———— 6. Colleagues will be more impressed with your past achievements if they learn about them from someone else, rather than from you.

———— ———— 7. Experience is a great teacher.

———— ———— 8. All supervisors have had an abundance of formal education.

———— ———— 9. It is asking too much of new employees to play down their expertise until they have built strong relationships with others.

———— ———— 10. In the work environment, productivity is more important than previous educational achievements.

SCORE ☐

Answers 1. T; 2. F; 3. T; 4. T; 5. F; 6. T; 7. T; 8. F; 9. F; 10. T.

It is up to each new employee to decide when and how to provide the technical skills or expertise that they possess. Sometimes these are needed immediately. At other times, it will take a few days before they can be introduced effectively. Most of the time, it is best to learn from others and then weave your own ideas (and expertise) into your work output. Whatever the situation, to antagonise others is counter-productive.

37

First-week assessment scale

This exercise is a personal progress report, designed to help you pinpoint areas of success and areas where renewed emphasis is needed. Do not complete it until you have been on your new job a full week. Tick the appropriate box – be totally honest with yourself.

	FULLY SATISFIED	PARTIALLY SATISFIED	NOT SATISFIED
Did I take advantage of learning opportunities?	☐	☐	☐
Did I avoid making too many first-week mistakes?	☐	☐	☐
How was my application of job skills?	☐	☐	☐
My grooming?	☐	☐	☐
My level of concentration	☐	☐	☐
My success at remembering names?	☐	☐	☐
How were my first-week listening skills?	☐	☐	☐
Did my personal work output improve	☐	☐	☐
Did I make a good impression on my fellow-workers?	☐	☐	☐
On my supervisor?	☐	☐	☐

Based on my answers, I intend to concentrate on improving the following areas next week:

1. _____
2. _____
3. _____
4. _____
5. _____

What do I need to learn next week?

Has your supervisor or colleague assigned to 'show you the ropes' given you any learning tasks? What have you observed that you will need to learn in the future? What do you want to learn next week?

To demonstrate your initiative and stay ahead of what your supervisor expects you to learn, list those tasks you wish to become better at next week. List them in the order in which you want to learn them.

1. _____

2. _____

3. _____

4. _____

5. _____

Psychologically it is often motivating to reward yourself for reaching short-term learning goals. Promise yourself a reward (dinner out? new article of clothing? sporting event?) if you reach your goals next week.

CHAPTER 3

Week Two:
Moving Ahead with Confidence

Second-week productivity

It is customary for new employees to use the second week on the job to get personal work output as close to standard (or the average of other employees) as possible.

```
PRODUCTIVITY SCALE

┌─────────────────────┐
│  - - - - - - - - -  │   Your potential productivity level
│                     │
│                     │   Departmental norm
│                     │
│                     │
│   Second Week       │
└─────────────────────┘   Starting level
```

Let's assume that you made satisfactory progress during your first week, but you recognise that you need to demonstrate measurable growth in your second. What strategy should you follow? There are three that you might consider.

Strategy 1   Go all out to get the level of your work output up to that of your fellow-workers. If necessary, cut down on socialising. Be friendly and pleasant, but let your job concentration do the talking.

Strategy 2   Announce to fellow-workers that your goal for the week is to get your output up to their level. Do this in a good-natured way and suggest that they keep an eye on your progress. Let them know that suggestions from them are welcome!

Strategy 3 Silently concentrate on your work output but do not neglect human relations. Strive for balance between the two and, if necessary, give yourself an additional week to reach the level of your fellow-workers.

In some situations (where you are finding it easy to reach productivity standards) you might concentrate on human relations. This is a good approach when you realise you can surpass the productivity of others but you do not want them to feel threatened by your ability.

How to handle embarrassing moments

Few things can be more embarrassing than to fail at something you have been trained to do well. For example, imagine the embarrassment of an English graduate who misspells a word in a letter in his first week in the job, or an accountant who makes a mistake in simple arithmetic.

Mistakes due to lack of experience can be embarrassing, too. You might have to give change to customers when you've never done it before, or you might be faced with equipment you've never used before.

'Ten years ago I was accepted on a management training course by a chain of restaurants. My first assignment was to operate the cash register. A hostess was assigned to help me, but I was more interested in her than her instructions. Result? I made so many stupid mistakes that I had to be retrained in front of everyone by the one person I was trying to impress – the manager.'

Countless other mistakes can happen in any new job. One way to minimise mistakes is through self-training. Here are a few suggestions:

- Admit your lack of experience if you have not had the required training.

- Position yourself so you can both hear the trainer/teacher and see the mechanics involved. Ask questions.

- Ask to do a dry run for any new procedure.

- Do new tasks step by step at your own speed until you become comfortable.

- If necessary, accept more help.

- Do not be afraid to ask for retraining. Find out who you should approach to receive it.

Everyone makes mistakes. When it happens to you, keep your sense of humour. Learn to laugh at yourself, and others will respect you. The biggest mistake is to assume you know how to do something before you really do, so that you make the same mistake again and again. Making a mistake in your first week is expected. Making the same mistake in the second and third weeks is not and will not enhance your image.

Coping with skill deficiencies

What happens if the first assignment you are given requires a skill above your level of experience? The following suggestions should help:

- Ask your supervisor to assign a colleague to assist you in getting your skill level higher.
- Cancel your plans for the next few nights so that you can improve your skills by staying late at work or practising elsewhere.
- Pay for some immediate classes (for example, at a local college).

It is a mistake to try and hide your skill level from others. Admitting you need help can often turn out to be an icebreaker with fellow-employees. They may have been in the same position themselves earlier. Once you receive on-the-job guidance it is important to demonstrate that you have benefited and that your skill performance has improved. To strengthen relationships with those who have 'bailed you out', wait for an opportunity to do something of importance for them so that they fully understand how much you appreciated their help when you needed it the most.

It may be possible for your manager to arrange for you to upgrade your skills by arriving early or staying late. Asking if this is possible demonstrates a good learning attitude.

Upgrading a skill takes time. Make sure your other job responsibilities are not neglected. In fact, it may be temporarily possible to offset the lack of skill in one area by contributing more in another where you are proficient. Perhaps an arrangement could be made with a colleague.

Give yourself 30 days to improve as many skills as possible. If you need more help, tell your supervisor what you are doing to improve your situation. Compensate for slow skill development by developing good human relations. It is your total contribution to the organisation that will eventually be measured.

Improving your job skills

Each job has its unique skill requirements. Some job skills (waitress, equipment operator, etc) can be taught from scratch after you have started work. Most jobs, however, require a certain skill level before employment is offered (computer operator, carpenter, etc). In all cases, new employees are required to either improve or adjust their existing skills.

Company sources

Supervisor   Your boss is responsible for your training and job performance. He or she may or may not give you the training you need. Some supervisors are outstanding instructors. Good luck!

Sponsor   It is a common and good practice for a supervisor to assign a sponsor (colleague) to you

	to train and guide you through your first few weeks.
Training	If you were fortunate enough to receive induction training, it was probably organised by the department. Check to see what other training is available and if your organisation provides correspondence courses, self-help books, etc.

External sources

Adult Education Centres	These run a variety of courses lasting from one term to a year or more, either one day, or one or more evenings per week during term time.
Colleges of Further Education	Colleges run part-time courses – day release, block release, evening classes or a combination – many leading to vocational and national diplomas and specialist certificates (eg CGLI, RSA, BTEC).
Open College	Runs short correspondence courses together with personal tuition, TV and radio backup, many relating to practical and work skills.
Correspondence Courses	There are various correspondence courses (apart from those offered by the Open College) that provide useful self-help programmes.

Self-help

Equipment Suppliers	Computer manufacturers often provide training manuals and software to teach their system or programme.
Libraries	Libraries are a good source of self-help manuals and books. A number of self-study books are included in the list of further reading on page 77.

Whatever local sources are available, it is the responsibility of the new employee to bring his or her skills up to standard and beyond.

Your communication style

It is vital that you speak up clearly and concisely in your new job. It is also important that any forms, notes or memos are written in your best handwriting, printed or typed. People need to hear and understand what you mean. If your English is weak (perhaps a second language), seek assistance.

The manner or style in which you communicate initially may be different from your normal style and from the way you will communicate later. Why is this? In most cases your approach will be conservative because you feel this style will help you to win the acceptance of colleagues. Later, you can relax and communicate in your own way.

How communicative should you be at first? Just enough to be friendly and get your tasks done? If you are not open, will people feel you are withdrawn and hard to get to know? How much communication is enough but not too much for your first days?

There are many factors involved (especially your particular work environment), but here are two styles you might consider on a temporary basis:

Style 1 Be quieter than usual. Concentrate on the work. Be very polite. Ask questions only when necessary. Communicate primarily with your attitude and job performance instead of with your voice. Do not worry if you appear nervous to others.

Style 2 Be modestly assertive. Call people by their first names if appropriate. Speak with confidence but be careful not to dominate conversations. Show your positive learning attitude by asking more questions than necessary. Be friendly and open. When appropriate, get others to laugh.

The following exercise is designed to get you thinking about how important communication will be to your success during the first few weeks. Your best strategy, of course, is the one that you feel most comfortable with and will build the best relationships with others. It's up to you to decide!

Show your preference for Style 1 or Style 2 by answering the following questions.

	Style 1	Style 2
As a long-term employee, which style would you react to best in a newcomer?	☐	☐
Which of the two styles comes closest to your natural style?	☐	☐
Which style would help a new employee to make the most progress in the first 30 days?	☐	☐
As a supervisor, which style would you prefer a new employee to use?	☐	☐

Teasing and testing

To be an outsider one day and an insider the next without a little teasing or testing may be asking too much. Fellow-workers often enjoy a joke at the expense of the newcomer. Some supervisors like to see how a new employee handles a difficult assignment.

Teasing is when fellow-workers have a little fun at your expense.

When Judy reported to work on her second week, she was told by a colleague to fax a copy of her CV (the one she used to get her job) to the head office in London. Judy did this without question and the reply from London was 'looks interesting, suggest she visits the office for an interview if she plans a trip to London'. This response brought a good laugh!

Because Judy was able to laugh about it herself, her relationship with her colleagues took a giant step forward. The laughter was, in a sense, a form of acceptance.

Testing is a more serious matter, and it is important to know the difference between the two. Where teasing is usually harmless, testing may indicate resentment, jealousy or even fear.

When Howard was assigned to Mr G for training, things didn't go well. He was given tasks to perform without being told how to do them. Then he was reprimanded for being slow. After two days, Howard knew something was seriously wrong, so he walked into Mr G's office seeking an explanation. To his surprise, Mr G quickly apologised, saying: 'I thought you were sent to replace me, and I was going to be out of a job. I decided to give you a hard time, hoping you would resign. But I've just learned that I have been promoted to a new job. So I will drop everything now and give you all the training you need. Sorry!

Sometimes a new employee is tested by a fellow-worker for unexplained, personal reasons. At other times, testing may occur when a fellow-worker feels that you are getting advantages she or he did not receive as a new employee. If, as a new employee, you find the testing is persistent (not just a temporary reaction), two actions are recommended. First, confront the person who keeps testing you and ask why. Second, discuss the matter with your supervisor. If it is the supervisor who is doing the testing and you judge it to be unfair, you have no choice but to discuss the matter with him or her. If the testing doesn't stop, you should talk to your supervisor's superior.

Protocol

Protocol means those courtesies, manners, and procedures considered proper in dealing with people within an organisation. Protocol describes the unwritten rules that colleagues and managers expect you to follow in certain situations. In most cases, you learn protocol after you have been in the job for a short time.

Such matters as the length of coffee breaks, the number of sick days allowed and similar rules are covered in staff manuals and can be learnt quickly. But a lot of protocol is not written out. For example, in most organisations it is a mistake to go over the head of your supervisor to discuss problems of importance to your department. This violates protocol because it undermines the supervisor's authority.

The following list describes areas where sensitivity is required. Tick any item that you feel would apply to your new job.

I plan to be sensitive when:

☐ Asking questions of my superiors.

☐ Setting up a communications session with my boss.

☐ Keeping my business and personal life separate.

☐ Talking in a negative manner about fellow employees.

☐ Discussing business details in a crowded lift.

☐ Using first names.

☐ Speaking or laughing in a loud voice that disturbs others.

☐ Telling jokes or stories that might offend others.

☐ Eavesdropping.

☐ Dressing in a manner that consistently distracts others from their productivity.

☐ _____

Protocol applies to delicate matters in which you have a choice of behaviour. You can act in a courteous, sensitive manner, or in a way that might embarrass others and make good relationships difficult. Of course, protocol is just as important after being in the job for a while as it is during your first few days. The big difference is that more people will watch your behaviour more closely at the beginning.

Improving working habits

Some typical bad habits are listed below. Place a tick next to those you want to avoid.

☐ Keeping a messy desk or work area.

☐ Turning in a poorly written report.

☐ Making a poor job of personal time management.

☐ Not being well groomed (grubby fingernails, uncombed hair, dirty shoes).

☐ Making or receiving too many personal telephone calls.

☐ Presenting a negative attitude to others when you really feel positive inside.

☐ Not taking good care of company equipment.

☐ Being late for work or for appointments.

☐ Making promises that you can't keep.

☐ Putting quantity before quality.

If you are starting your first career job after leaving college, you have a golden opportunity to form good working habits. The same is true if you are entering the workplace after an absence. But if you have built up an inventory of bad habits in your previous job, you have a major challenge. You must leave those habits behind and learn new ones.

Whatever the case, here are three reminders:

● It is much easier to eliminate bad working habits when you enter a new environment.

● In your desire to be accepted by fellow-workers, do not pick up their bad habits to add to your own.

● If you have a habit or mannerism that irritates others in your personal life, it will probably be twice as offensive to fellow-workers.

Developing good working habits is the professional way!

Case Study 2
Unprepared

It is Saturday morning and David is looking back on his second week with Ace Tech. Everyone has been helpful and friendly and David feels proud to be associated with such an impressive group of professionals. But he is very concerned over what happened just before he left work on Friday. His superior, Jane Shafer, called him into her office and said he would replace Alice Redley as head of the Credit Control Department, starting on Monday morning.

Although David has an accountancy degree and computer skills, he's worried that Ms Shafer may be assuming he is more qualified and experienced than he really is. Without meaning to, she may be leading him to failure. David is not familiar with the type of computers used, or the sales ledger system at Ace. As far as he can tell, when Monday morning arrives he will be on his own.

List what you think David should do over the weekend to prepare himself better for Monday morning.

_____

_____

_____

What should David do on arriving at work on Monday morning?

_____

_____

_____

Compare your thoughts with those of the author by turning to page 75.

What do I need to learn next week?

What success did you achieve in reaching your learning goals last week? Did you reward yourself as planned? If circumstances were such that you weren't able to learn everything you planned, try again next week. Feel free to add any learning tasks you listed last week (but were unable to learn) and also list some new ones. In addition, add any learning tasks you have been assigned by others.

Second-week assessment scale

This exercise is designed to help you evaluate your progress after two weeks in your new job. Tick the appropriate box. Honesty with yourself will guarantee you a better future!

	FULLY SATISFIED	PARTIALLY SATISFIED	NOT SATISFIED
How is my learning progress after two weeks?	☐	☐	☐
How is my progress in building good relationships with fellow-workers?	☐	☐	☐
How am I doing in closing my personal productivity gap?	☐	☐	☐
How do I rate my patience with others?	☐	☐	☐
Am I building a strong relationship with my supervisor?	☐	☐	☐
How do I feel about my personal confidence?	☐	☐	☐
What about my ability to relax and enjoy my work?	☐	☐	☐
Do I remain positive in all situations?	☐	☐	☐
How are my health and energy levels?	☐	☐	☐
How do I feel about myself?	☐	☐	☐

Based on my answers, I intend to concentrate on making improvements in the following areas next week:

1. _____

2. _____

3. _____

4. _____

5. _____

1. _____
2. _____
3. _____
4. _____
5. _____

Think of a way to reward yourself if you reach all your goals next week.

CHAPTER 4
Week Three:
Strengthening Relationships

Third-week productivity

The chances are that by now your work output is up to your own, and your supervisor's expectations. If it isn't, you should discuss the matter with your supervisor so that retraining or other adjustments can be made.

Let's assume, however, that you are up to the standard of your fellow-workers, and you feel that you can start to move ahead of that standard. In other words, you can continue to close the gap between your present productivity and your potential.

How should you go about doing this?
Carefully is the key word, because you want to continue strengthening relationships while improving your output. You want your extra productivity to inspire others to do better themselves – not to turn them against you because they feel you are showing them up.

When Steve knew his work output was at least average in the department, he decided to go full speed ahead to gain the attention of his supervisor and, he hoped, put himself in line for a quick promotion. Result? Steve turned his fellow-workers against him and his supervisor found it necessary to give him a 'teamwork approach to productivity' lecture.

Many new employees fail to see that they also contribute to productivity when they make it more comfortable for their fellow-workers to produce. Steve, despite his high potential, did not sense the overall picture until his superior spelt it out to him.

Don't let this happen to you!
Your strategy should be to increase your personal work output in such a way that your fellow-employees support your efforts and are motivated to follow you. This is the only way in which you can make your maximum contribution to your department. It is also the best strategy to use in preparing yourself for a future position as a supervisor.

What if you have a difficult supervisor?

Just as there are problem colleagues, there are also difficult supervisors. Some are excessively demanding; some have little patience; others find it difficult to communicate. Regardless of the kind of supervisor you get, it is vital that you build the best possible relationship with this person. How do you do this? There are two major factors for immediate consideration:

1. **React to the management style of your supervisor,** not to his or her personality. All supervisors develop a unique way of operating. Your challenge is to adjust to this style and ignore individual traits or mannerisms (voice, expressions, physical features, manner of dress, other peculiarities). In other words, look past your supervisor's personality to what he or she is trying to accomplish.

2. **Concentrate on productivity and relationships with fellow-workers** as you learn to work in harmony with your supervisor. Who knows – your supervisor may be staying neutral until it is known how productive you are and how effectively you work with others. Above all, do not let fellow-employees turn you against a supervisor who may eventually be your greatest supporter.

In addition, the following tips are suggested:

- Don't expect a perfect supervisor.
- Remember that supervisors are human and sometimes have bad days.
- Select the right time to ask questions.
- Refuse to allow a small matter to turn into a major issue.
- Don't go above your supervisor's head, except as a last resort.
- If you make a mistake, tell your boss yourself. He or she should not hear about it from others.

It is far better to take the time to find out how to build a good relationship with a boss, than to judge him or her too quickly. Go carefully and give your superior a chance to find out just how professional you really can be!

Case Study 3
Choice

On Monday morning after two weeks in the job, Joyce was invited into the office of her supervisor, Ms Crane. Tense about the purpose of the meeting, Joyce was relieved when Ms Crane paid her a sincere compliment and told her that the employee Joyce was hired to replace was returning from leave sooner than expected. She told Joyce not worry because two other supervisors had requested her services. Best of all, Joyce could choose between the two assignments.

Department A is supervised by Mr King, a long-term employee. Department A has the reputation of promoting more employees into better jobs than any other department. Mr King is considered an outstanding teacher. However, he is highly authoritarian. In fact, he runs such a tight ship that his employee turnover is higher than that of any other supervisor in the company.

Department B is supervised by Ms Jones, a young manager recently out of college. This department has the reputation for getting a lot of work out of people, and they seem to enjoy doing it. Many workers envy those who work in Ms Jones's department. On the other hand, no one from her department has been promoted in the two years since Ms Jones became manager.

If you were Joyce, which department would you choose? Why?

_____

_____

_____

_____

_____

_____

_____

_____

_____

_____

To compare your answer with that of the author, turn to page 75.

Reinforcing relationships

After a couple of weeks in the job, you have had an opportunity to build a few new and rewarding relationships. Some were probably easier to build than others. You may not have been successful in all directions. This is natural, because some people are more reserved than others. And a few people present a special challenge because they do not quickly give their support to any newcomer. The good news is that once you build a good working relationship with these more reserved colleagues, it is likely to be a meaningful, lasting one.

List below the names of those fellow-workers you wish to build a strong relationship with but with whom you have had little success so far.

1. _____ 3. _____

2. _____ 4. _____

How are you going to develop a relationship with these particular colleagues and improve your relationship with others? Here are four suggestions:

1. Continue to maintain your work output and your image as a serious, professional worker.

2. Be generous with 'thank you's. Comments like these are appreciated: 'Thanks for making my first few weeks easier'; 'You have been a great help to me. Thanks'; 'Without your assistance settling in here would have been a lot less fun. Thanks for all your help.'

3. Continue to ask for advice – asking for advice is an excellent way to improve a relationship. For example: 'Could you tell me how to learn new features of the word-processing software?'; 'I've mastered most of my tasks but I am still having trouble with the reduction machine. Could you have a look to see what I am doing wrong?'

4. Pay more compliments. Don't wait any longer to pay sincere compliments, even to those who are holding back a little. For example: 'I wish I was as good on the telephone as you'; 'I'll never learn to match your speed'; 'I really appreciate your professionalism. I hope you don't mind if I try some of your techniques.'

Avoiding personal job stress

When specialists talk about job stress they are usually referring to the excessive pressure that some jobs create. This stress can lead to the mental and emotional exhaustion known as job 'burnout'.

It is is also possible to create unnecessary stress for yourself when you are in a new job. Sometimes new employees try so hard to succeed that they wear down their immune systems and catch a cold or develop a stress-related illness. How can you prevent this from happening?

Here are three suggestions:

1. **Regulate your work tempo.** When you move into a new environment, it is easy to succumb to the pressures that surround you. When you allow this to happen, your job performance goes down instead of up. Make sure you take all the breaks due to you and resist working outside working hours. Resist the pressure to speed up. Keep regular hours away from work for the first few weeks. Exercise on a daily basis. The phrase 'one day at a time' will never have more meaning to you.

2. **Learn to increase your performance daily, step by step.** Each new day in the job, increase your tempo a little without getting too excited and overdoing it. Learn to do one job at a time so you won't get frustrated trying to go in too many directions at once. Despite the many demands on you, develop your own pace. It may be necessary to discuss your progress with your supervisor to prevent your having to take on too many responsibilities too soon.

3. **Within limits, relax a little.** As a new employee, you will need the safety valve of laughter even more than others. Relax and enjoy the company of colleagues when the time is right. Initiate humour when appropriate. Allow the stress that does accumulate within you to escape.

The three Cs of office politics

When people work together, there will naturally be a variety of values, standards and cultural differences. In some environments, these differences can be seen in the form of office politics. When this happens, workers sometimes score points against each other, and the harmony desired by management disappears.

As a new member, you can be caught up in the winds and tides of politics, and this has the potential to damage your career. How do you avoid this? How can you stay clear? It may help to know about the three Cs of office politics: camps, cliques and critics.

1. Camps

Without knowing it, you may walk into a work environment that is divided into two or more camps. One camp might be pro-management, the other anti-. One camp might be pro-union, the other anti-. Or it is possible that one camp rallies round one worker, another camp round another. The danger, of course, is that you may be in the middle and intimidated into making a choice. What is the solution? Stay clear and chart a course down the middle.

2. Cliques

A clique can be seen as a small camp that does not have any opposition. Most cliques are composed of a small circle of people who like to stick together. This is evident during breaks. Cliques often appear exclusive or snobbish to other workers and your career will be better off if you do not join a clique, especially at first. The reason? Because the moment you join, you are taking sides. Your challenge is to get along equally with all employees. Here again, stay clear and chart a course so that both clique members and others respect you.

3. Critics

All organisations have a few critics among their employees. Many are experienced people who have become sidetracked into dead-end jobs. They love to convert newcomers to their negative views. How do you deal with a critic? Listen, be polite, but don't be taken in. And, above all, do not let yourself be over-identified with a critic.

Keep the three Cs in mind as you try to build good, sound, healthy working relationships with all the people in your work environment.

Case Study 4
Absenteeism

After a wonderful scuba-diving trip over the weekend, Kelly woke up on Monday morning with a high temperature and feeling miserable. It was only her third week in the new job (which she loves), but she knew she had to phone in to say she was ill so arrangements could be made for colleagues to cover for her. Kelly was also absent on Tuesday and Wednesday. Sensing she might be creating a problem for herself if she missed any more days, she went into work on Thursday and struggled through until the weekend.

When she reports to work the next Monday (almost fully recovered), everyone, including her supervisor, is friendly and sympathetic. So much so that she relaxes and talks about all the fun she had on her scuba trip, neglecting to thank those colleagues who covered for her. Although nothing is said, Kelly begins to notice some distance between her and her colleagues. They seem less eager to help her. Her supervisor appears more demanding.

Do you think Kelly's absenteeism damaged the start of her career? Why and where has the damage occurred? Can she repair the damage? How?

_____

_____

_____

_____

_____

_____

_____

_____

_____

See page 76 to compare your answer with that of the author.

Third-week assessment scale

Complete this assessment after you have been on the job three weeks.

	FULLY SATISFIED	PARTIALLY SATISFIED	NOT SATISFIED
Have I increased my work output to my best level?	☐	☐	☐
What about the quality of my work?	☐	☐	☐
How are my human relations skills?	☐	☐	☐
How is my punctuality and absentee record?	☐	☐	☐
Am I maintaining a good visual image?	☐	☐	☐
Have I reduced the number of mistakes I make at a fast enough pace?	☐	☐	☐
How are my verbal skills?	☐	☐	☐
Have I succeeded in not showing a negative attitude?	☐	☐	☐
Have I taken full advantage of all opportunities?	☐	☐	☐
How do I rate my professional growth and image so far?	☐	☐	☐

Based on my answers, I intend to concentrate on improving the following areas next week:

1. _____
2. _____
3. _____
4. _____
5. _____

What do I need to learn next week?

Your 30 days will soon be up, so it's time to concentrate on learning any tasks that are still a problem for you. Are there a few tasks you have neglected? Do you need to retrain yourself (or get special help) to achieve a learning goal that is giving you trouble? List below those remaining tasks (operating a machine, completing a special report, etc) that you wish to learn next week.

1. _____

2. _____

3. _____

4. _____

5. _____

If you feel really satisfied with your learning progress over the past three weeks and confident that you can accomplish most of the goals listed above, shouldn't you promise yourself a special reward?

CHAPTER 5

Week Four:
Improving Your Professionalism

Career countdown

Whatever your new job or new assignment happens to be, it should be considered as a launching pad to help you reach long-term career goals. In this respect a job is never just a job – it is an opportunity.

For individuals who prefer to work their way into better positions within the same organisation, it is not uncommon to occupy 20 or more different positions within a career period.

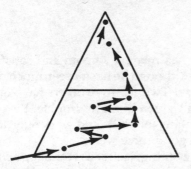

Top management

Middle management

Lower management

For those who elect to move from one firm to another as they zigzag their way to the top (see diagram overleaf), moves are made based upon the reputation they have created behind them.

Either way, there is much more at stake than the position you occupy when you start your career. Everything you learn can be used later on in more demanding positions.

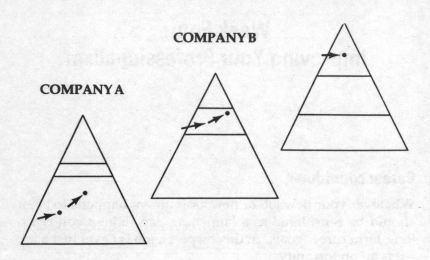

COMPANY C

COMPANY B

COMPANY A

Case Study 5
Premature?

As far as he can tell, Jack has made a smooth and satisfactory adjustment to his new job. Although he hasn't seen much of him, his supervisor seems happy. Two fellow-workers have ignored Jack, but the others haven't given him any trouble. Best of all, Jack has found it easy to get his job skills and work output up to par. All in all, it has been a good three weeks.

While driving home one evening, Jack starts thinking about the possibility of becoming a supervisor with his firm. 'After all,' he says to himself, 'if I can make so much progress in such a short period, what is to hold me back? I think I'll make an appointment with my supervisor tomorrow. I'll get his advice on what I need to do to qualify for his job or a similar one in another department.'

How do you think Jack's supervisor would answer? Write out your response on the following page.

_____
_____
_____
_____
_____
_____
_____
_____
_____
_____
_____

To compare your answer with that of the author, turn to page 76.

Misgivings

Interviews indicate that almost all new employees have down periods – a sudden flurry of doubts about whether they have made the right decision in accepting the new job or assignment. Just as when you have bought a new car, a temporary wave of remorse may occur. New employees frequently ask themselves questions such as:

What am I doing here?
Am I with the right organisation?
Can I learn everything they expect me to know?
Did I spend all that time at college for this?

Misgivings are natural and to be expected. They are part of the adjustment period. Sometimes, a simple little incident will trigger a down period.

Sarah sailed into her new job with confidence. Then one day, after completing a difficult customer transaction, she noticed her supervisor watching her with an air of dissatisfaction. That night, Sarah had trouble sleeping. But the next day the supervisor, sensing what might have occurred, told Sarah that she had handled things extremely well and that he was actually upset with the customer (a known complainer). Sarah's confidence quickly returned.

However, most doubts occur when new employees start to fear that they cannot upgrade their skills sufficiently to keep their positions. They are overwhelmed by how much they have to learn and temporarily forget that they have plenty of time in which to learn it. Usually, all it takes is a lunch break or a good night's sleep, and the misgivings disappear. Here are three tips that can help to speed up the confidence restoration process:

- If you start to feel the job may be too much for you, concentrate on your work output.

- If you feel rejected by fellow-workers, ask the one you respect the most to tell you what you may be doing wrong.

- Keep reminding yourself that Rome wasn't built in a day and that you have time in which to improve.

Balancing productivity and human relations

Your primary goal during your first 30 days should be to achieve the best possible balance between high productivity and good human relations. It is a goal that should remain with you throughout your career.

In the diagram on page 67, notice that the employee in the middle has increased his or her output to above average while at the same time establishing a strong relationship with the supervisor (vertical relationship) and good working relationships with two fellow-workers (horizontal relationships). Keeping the vertical and horizontal relationships at high levels, and in balance, is the key to career success.

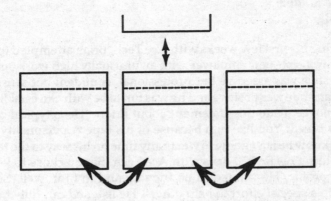

Once you achieve a good balance, your future challenge will be to improve and maintain it. Here are three suggestions:

1. **It is as dangerous to become sloppy in human relationships as it is in your job performance.** Keep reminding yourself that you contribute to departmental productivity in two ways – what you do and what others do, because you are a team-player.

2. **Do not resent others because you seem to carry more departmental productivity than they do.** You may be more ambitious than your fellow-employees, or you may have received better training elsewhere, or your potential may be higher.

3. **Helping others to reach their productivity potential can mean as much to your career as doing it yourself.** As you have learnt from those who assisted you, a good way to build a lasting relationship with a colleague is to help that person to succeed. Helping others is an excellent way to promote your career.

Become professional!
Stay professional!
Enjoy being professional!

Case Study 6
Style

During his first few weeks with Ace Tech, Brian attempted to be a highly visible new employee with an unusually high work output. His style was assertive but professional, confident but sensitive. His attitude was positive and he was fun to be with. An established employee made this statement about Brian. 'He is typical of the new breed. You like him because of his type A personality, but you know he isn't going to waste any time on his way to the top.'

During his first 30 days with Ace Tech, Simon chose to keep a low profile. He wanted to be friendly and to fit in well. Simon made a special effort to help others. He listened carefully before jumping in with suggestions. He worked hard to build sound relations with both colleagues and superiors. One fellow-employee said this of Simon: 'He is really a nice chap. In my opinion, he will eventually make a strong employee. I like his style. He has my support.'

Who, in your opinion, has made the most progress in 30 days, Brian or Simon? Who has been the most professional?

_____

_____

_____

_____

_____

_____

_____

_____

_____

Turn to page 76 to compare your answer with that of the author.

Fourth-week assessment

Although you may have been sharing your experiences informally with friends, now that you are completing your first month it might make sense to talk over your experiences more seriously with a friend, spouse, mentor or adviser. You might consider the following:

Have things turned out in the way you envisaged?
Has this book helped? How?
What has happened to your image both at work and away from work?
Do you have more confidence than when you started your job?
What would you do differently the next time you start a new job or move into a new working environment?
Do you consider yourself a stronger person now?
Has there been any permanent improvement in your learning attitude? Your attitude in general?
If the person (or persons) you choose to talk to were to start a new job, would you suggest using this book?

Talking over these questions with the right person could help reinforce what you have learned, and help you to crystallise your thoughts for the future.

In addition to talking things over, you might enjoy testing yourself on what you have learned. If so, complete the self-marking quiz that follows.

Demonstrate your progress
For each statement, put a tick under True or False.

TRUE	FALSE	
————	————	1. What you have learnt in your new job about being a more comfortable person to meet will probably not help you in other social situations.

———— ———— 2. Most career professionals would find it embarrassing to take notes in front of others.

———— ———— 3. Although there is always a gap between one's productivity level and one's potential, the smaller the gap the better.

———— ———— 4. It is possible to compensate for a lack of formal education and experience by having a superior learning attitude.

———— ———— 5. As a new employee, the best way to build good relationships with colleagues is to make sure your work output is well above average during your first few days.

———— ———— 6. Practising good human relations is the best way to overcome deficiencies in productive skills.

———— ———— 7. New employees who have come from another job have an advantage over first-time employees when it comes to establishing good working habits.

———— ———— 8. You should react to the personality of the supervisor and not to his or her management style.

———— ———— 9. Knowing the three Cs of office politics reminds the new employee to play it safe and build good relationships with all fellow-workers.

———— ———— 10. At the beginning of a new experience, humility and a good learning attitude go together.

SCORE ☐

Answers 1. False (it should be a big help). 2. False (just the opposite). 3. True. 4. True. 5. False (any increase in productivity should be accompanied by some human relation efforts). 6. False (but human relations can help until the deficiency is corrected). 7. False (those who come from other jobs usually have bad habits that need correcting). 8. False. 9. True. 10. True.

CHAPTER 6
Final Review

Be true to your future

Whatever has been your experience in the past few weeks, two primary learning goals remain.

Learning goal 1 It is vital that you sit down and review your strengths and weaknesses using the form provided.

When filling in your form, you may wish to look back through this book (especially the assessment pages) to get a better idea of your learning progress.

You could also ask your supervisor to assess your progress, and take note of any criticisms or suggestions.

Learning goal 2 What kind of training will you need in the future? Should you undertake more formal training? How much can you continue to learn on the job? Will you be able to maintain your professional learning attitude as your career progresses?

To assist you in answering these and similar questions, complete the exercise 'Consolidating your gains' on page 73.

30-day assessment

This assessment form is designed to be a significant part of *Making an Impact in Your New Job*. (It does not replace other organisational performance assessments.)

In evaluating your performance, circle the number most applicable. A 10, 9 or 8 highly acceptable. A 7, 6, 5 or 4 is acceptable. A 3 or less is not acceptable.

	Highly Acceptable	Acceptable	Not Acceptable
Contribution to productivity during the first few days	10 9 8	7 6 5 4	3 2 1
Quality of relationship with colleagues	10 9 8	7 6 5 4	3 2 1
Skill improvement demonstrated	10 9 8	7 6 5 4	3 2 1
Absenteeism	10 9 8	7 6 5 4	3 2 1
Attitude	10 9 8	7 6 5 4	3 2 1
Willingness to learn	10 9 8	7 6 5 4	3 2 1
Communication skills	10 9 8	7 6 5 4	3 2 1
Professional image	10 9 8	7 6 5 4	3 2 1
Potential for growth	10 9 8	7 6 5 4	3 2 1
Participation as a team-member	10 9 8	7 6 5 4	3 2 1

TOTAL SCORE

Consolidating your gains

In your first 30 days in the job, your knowledge should have expanded. Most of what you have learnt has probably come from on-the-job experience. But you have also gained knowledge, principles and techniques from other sources.

How can you organise, consolidate and put in order of priority what you have learnt so that it will mean more to you in the future?

Listed below are 10 aspects of life at work. If you decide which areas you have made the most progress in, you will know where you excel. If you locate a few areas where you need extra growth to enhance your career, you will know where to concentrate your learning in the future.

Read all 10 areas, then write the number 1 in the box where you feel your most excel. Write the number 2 in the box by the area that comes next, and continue until you have written a 10 where you need the most help.

☐ Communication: all aspects (with superiors, colleagues, family, friends)

☐ Job skills: staying ahead of others in job competencies

☐ Human relations: building strong relationships with colleagues, superiors, customers, etc

☐ Productivity: keeping work output close to my potential and above the norm

☐ Self-management: making the best use of time, preventing burnout, balancing home and career, management of personal finances, etc

☐ Attitude: being able to stay positive during stressful times; bouncing back quickly

☐ Image: maintaining a professional image in all my career contacts

☐ Management skills: Do I aspire to a career in management? Do I have potential? What training have I had?

☐ Quality: Do I maintain the highest possible standards of excellence?

☐ Confidence: Am I sufficiently assertive or do I back away from confrontations?

For future growth, you should concentrate on the areas you designated as 6, 7, 8, 9 and 10.

Suggested Answers to Case Studies

1. Rescue
It would appear that Sandra may have been rejected by fellow-workers and is getting back at them by trying to turn Pat against them. Pat should take her time in making her own assessment of her fellow-workers. If she and Sandra become too close too soon, others in the department may not give Pat a chance to get to know them. Pat needs to get to know everyone on an equal basis. She should tell Sandra she is too busy for after-work refreshments and that she will see her tomorrow. A close relationship with Sandra may do Pat more harm than good.

2. Unprepared
David should go to the local library (or look at his student textbooks) to revise his knowledge of credit control. If possible, he should also spend some time on the kind of computer he will be using. On Monday morning, David should arrive early and ask Ms Shafer to assign someone to 'show him the ropes'. If this isn't possible, he should ask those in the department for help and assistance.

3. Choice
Joyce should get as much additional information from Ms Crane as possible. In fact, her advice could be crucial to the choice Joyce makes, because she has had a chance to observe Joyce at work for two weeks. If Joyce decides that learning more and getting promoted sooner is more important than

being in a happy environment, she should go for Mr King. On the other hand, happy employees are often better motivated. Ms Jones's style as a supervisor might act as a model for Joyce, and this might enhance her career more than if she went to Mr King.

4. Absenteeism

It may be unfair, but being absent within the first 30 days of a new job is usually more damaging than it would be later on. This is because the new employee has yet to prove her worth, and may still be a question mark in the minds of others. Kelly compounded the problem by talking about her fun weekend and by not thanking colleagues for helping with the workload. The damage has been to Kelly's image as a responsible person. She can repair the damage, but it will take time.

5. Premature?

Jack's performance may have been enough to get him off to a fair start. But he has underestimated what it takes to be a successful employee, let alone a manager. Jack has not taken full advantage of his learning opportunities during the first three weeks, and it shows in his attitude.

6. Style

In the author's view, there is not much to choose between Brian and Simon. In some environments, Brian would make more progress; in others, Simon would come out ahead. There is less risk to Simon's style, because his lower-key approach is less apt to turn others against him. Also, if Simon stays in the same department, he may overtake Brian because of stronger support from colleagues.

Further Reading from Kogan Page

How to Choose a Career, Vivien Donald
How to Communicate Effectively, Bert Decker
How to Develop a Positive Attitude, Elwood N Chapman
How to Get More Done, John and Fiona Humphrey
Make Every Minute Count, Marion E Haynes
Managing Your Time, Lothar J Seiwert
Memory Skills in Business: Basic Techniques for Improvement, Madelyn Burley-Allen
A Practical Guide to Effective Listening, Diane Bone
Returning to Work: A Practical Guide for Women, Alec Reed
The School Leaver's Handbook, Ann Jones
Study Skills Strategies: How to Learn More in Less Time, Uelaine Lengefeld
Successful Self-Management: A Sound Approach to Personal Effectiveness, Paul R Timm